# NOLS
## Backcountry
## Cooking

D1479074

0  11557 03464  6

# NOLS
## Backcountry
## Cooking

*Creative Menu Planning
for Short Trips*

Edited by Claudia Pearson
and Joanne Kuntz

STACKPOLE
BOOKS

Published by
STACKPOLE BOOKS
5067 Ritter Road
Mechanicsburg, PA 17055
www.stackpolebooks.com

Printed in the United States of America

First edition

10  9  8  7  6  5  4  3  2  1

*Cover design by Caroline Stover*
*Cover photograph by Brad Christensen*

**Library of Congress Cataloging-in-Publication Data**
  NOLS backcountry cooking : creative menu planning for
short trips / edited by Claudia Pearson and Joanne Kuntz ;
Illustrations by Mike Clelland. — 1st ed.
        p. cm.
  Includes index.
  ISBN-13: 978-0-8117-3464-6
  ISBN-10: 0-8117-3464-1
  1.  Outdoor cookery. 2.  Menus. I.  Pearson, Claudia, 1955–
II.  Kuntz, Joanne. III.  National Outdoor Leadership
School (U.S.)

TX823.N63 2008
641.5'78—dc22

                                                      2007023698

# Contents

# About NOLS

With the goal of training leaders to serve the growing number of people using the wilderness, Paul Petzoldt and Tap Tapley led the first NOLS expedition, an educational journey into wild land that started on June 8, 1965. Spanning over four decades, NOLS graduates now number more than 80,000 from around the world. The mission of NOLS (and Paul's original dream) abides still in an educational organization rooted in extended wilderness expeditions. Students travel away from civilization into mountains, deserts, and oceans, into heat and cold, to learn the skills they need to run their own expeditions and to lead others.

Lessons in team building, self-confidence, problem solving, sound judgment, and overall competence (including, yes, cooking) are a part of all NOLS courses. The leadership qualities gained last long after the course ends and are readily adaptable to life this side of the trailhead.

NOLS promotes protection of its wilderness classrooms through environmental education and stewardship, reaching out to larger audiences by way of research, seminars, short specialized courses, and publications.

In a world that humans like to think they dominate, the lessons learned from direct experience with nature are, as they have always been, of the utmost importance. If anything, those lessons are even more important today. The staff at NOLS seeks to be open to those lessons as individuals, to apply them to life and to the management of the school, and to make them available to the world community.

Wilderness, education, leadership, safety, community, and excellence—these values define and direct NOLS. For more information call (800) 710-NOLS or visit us at www.nols.edu.

# Introduction

You might be one of the many thousands who have digested *NOLS Cookery*, a detailed presentation of the National Outdoor Leadership School's (NOLS) bulk rationing system that has fed more people over the past forty plus years than some small nations. The bulk rationing system, in case you sit unaware, provides every cook group (usually two to four participants) with a wide selection of bulk foods and spices. Each group decides what to cook at each meal with the help of *NOLS Cookery* and knowledgeable peers or instructors. There are no set menus, and you learn, on a NOLS course, the art of cooking in the field. The system works wonderfully well for large groups on multiweek expeditions, but smaller groups going out for shorter lengths of time— five days or less—might want to consider menu planning instead. With the menu planning system, all meals are determined in advance, and the food purchased and packed accordingly. And so you hold in your hand *NOLS Backcountry Cooking: Creative Menu Planning for Short Trips,* written to answer this question: "How do I plan food for a short trip with a few friends and still maintain the NOLS culinary experience?"

You could supply the food for a wilderness trip by stopping by your favorite outdoor specialty shop, or even one of the many massive buy-it-all-here stores, and stocking up on freeze-dried fare. You will not suffer nutritionally after two to five days of rehydrated pasta primavera, but prepackaged freeze-dried food jacks up the expense of a trip quite a ways beyond the menu planning system. More importantly to us, you will miss an opportunity to experience not only real and creative cooking in the field but also the delights of the camp kitchen without undue stress on your time management plan.

Why is that important to us? At NOLS we embrace the total outdoor living experience. Eating is far more than wolfing down a pot of energy for the upcoming miles of trail or river. Cooking is an essential outdoor skill, like traveling safely on durable surfaces and setting up a comfortable and environmentally-friendly camp. Cooking becomes a social event, and the camp kitchen, approached thoughtfully and creatively, is anticipated, relished, and bound to generate many lasting and happy memories. Yes, the menu planning system consumes more time than eat-and-run meal plans. But we believe, with all our hearts and stomachs, it is time very well spent.

# Plan to
## SUCCEED

Food is fuel, yes, but food can and should also be fun. Who wants to end an invigorating day of hiking or paddling with a bowl of tasteless noodles or bland rehydrated beans? Only the unenlightened or the uneducated. Read on— and be neither.

# Menu
# PLANNING

The menu planning system does not involve rocket science. It does involve simplicity and convenience without a heavy burden on your bank account. Most of the thinking happens before you ever leave home, and that means you arrive at your campsite able to prepare a tasty and nourishing meal without spending unnecessary time and energy on food prep in the field. Menu planning is ideal for short trips, and we have focused on two- to five-day trips. We will run through the steps here via a sample menu plan for a three-day, two-night trip for three people.

## THE STEPS OF THE MENU PLANNING SYSTEM

### Step 1
*Determine the number of meals you will need for the duration of your trip*—the number of break-

# The Steps of the Menu Planning System

**Step 1:** Determine the number of meals you will need for the duration of your trip.

**Step 2:** Decide specifically what you will eat at each of your meals.

**Step 3:** Estimate how much food you will need at each meal to feed the number of people going on the trip.

**Step 4:** Determine the total needed food poundage based on your menu, and generate a shopping list based on the types and weights of food you would like to buy.

**Step 5:** Go shopping for the grub.

**Step 6:** Repackage, prep, and pack your food for the trip.

fasts, lunches, and dinners. All you need, so far, is to know when you are leaving and when you are returning home. For our purposes, let's say you want to leave work early on Friday for a two-hour drive to the trailhead and return Sunday evening. You will need two dinners (Friday and Saturday), two breakfasts (Saturday and Sunday), and two lunches (Saturday and Sunday).

**Step 2**
*Decide specifically what you will eat at each of your meals.* We have included A Quick Look at Food Ideas here and recipes in their own section to help you think creatively about cooking in the backcountry and learn about the versatility of all these foods.

With tortillas, instant beans, cheese, and salsa you can whip up a warm, fresh-tasting dinner in the time it takes to raise water to the boiling point.

Or purchase a few varieties of dinner-in-a-package such as Lipton dinners with choices such as Rice & Sauce (the Creamy Chicken is good) or Pasta & Sauce (great Creamy Garlic). It takes about ten minutes of boiling, and the manufacturers suggest adding milk (powdered

## Dry Yer Own

Food dryers are a wonderful addition to any kitchen. They are available in most hardware, discount, or kitchen supply stores. A large variety of homegrown or store-bought fresh vegetables, fruits, and meats can be dried, providing tasty, affordable, and nutritious additions to a backpacker's menu. There are many books available on drying and dehydrating foods at the local library. You can even dry foods in your own oven.

works fine) and butter or margarine. You do not have to add the milk and/or margarine, but it surely tastes better. For more wholesome options, check out Near East 100% Natural dishes such as Couscous with Toasted Pine

## Thoughts on Shopping

If you are responsible for shopping for the food for a trip, take note of the food preferences and allergies within your group, and purchase accordingly. Practice proper expedition behavior by not letting your personal likes and dislikes influence all your choices. Variety is the spice of life. If you need to, you can balance more expensive purchases with less expensive purchases by establishing a predetermined budget.

Nuts or Whole Grain Wheat Pilaf—or try Lundberg products such as Creamy Parmesan Risotto (eco-farmed, low-fat, gluten-free).

For the first day or so, you can pack in fresh foods: fruits (an apple for lunch) and vegetables (an onion to add flavor and nutrition to dinner). Meat that starts the day frozen in your pack will be ready to cook at dinner.

Although freeze-dried food will not be the basis of your menu plan, a few items (some available in bulk from NOLS) can add a lot of tasty nutrition to your meals: freeze-dried peas, for instance, rehydrated in a pasta dish, or freeze-dried beans in a tortilla.

Using suggestions from this book, your weekend menu plan could look like this:

| FRIDAY | SATURDAY | SUNDAY |
|---|---|---|
| | **Breakfast** | **Breakfast** |
| | Granola | Bagels (fried) |
| | Milk | Pepper jack cheese |
| | Cowboy Coffee | Summer sausage |
| | *(recipe page 74)* | Cowboy Coffee |
| | **Lunch** | **Lunch** |
| | Summer sausage | Peanut butter |
| | Bagels | Crackers |
| | Havarti cheese | GORP *(recipe page 96)* |
| | GORP | Fruit drink |
| | Fruit drink | |
| **Dinner** | **Dinner** | |
| Instant soup | Fried Rice *(recipe page 82)* | |
| Gado-Gado | Green peas | |
| Spaghetti | No-Bake Eskimo | |
| *(recipe page 78)* | Cookies *(recipe page 96)* | |
| Fruit bars | Hot chocolate | |
| Hot chocolate | | |

Pick and choose, mix and match, or save room for your personal preferences.

# A Quick Look at Food Ideas

**Nitty-Gritty Necessities**

- **Cheese:** a necessary staple in the backcountry. When in doubt, add cheese. Cheddar, Swiss, jack, mozzarella, and Parmesan work well on the trail.
- **Salt & pepper:** the minimalist's spice kit
- **Margarine, butter, and/or oil:** good for sautéing or frying and adding calories for energy-packed meals
- **Powdered milk (just add cold water):** useful in many recipes and beverages
- **Sugar:** brown or white

**Breakfast Basics and Beyond**

- **Hot cereals.** Cream of Wheat, rice, rye cereal, oatmeal, and hominy grits are all examples of hot cereals and are available in many forms: regular or instant, in bulk or individual packets. Some

*Breakfast*

cereals come presweetened; others can be mixed with sugar, dried fruits, nuts, milk, and margarine for breakfast. Cereals such as oatmeal can be added to dishes served for dinner meals. Grits may be cooked and allowed to sit for a while before serving. They can then be refried and served with hot sauce, lots of cheese, and pepper.

- **Cold cereals.** Granola, muesli, raisin bran, or any name-brand boxed cereal can be eaten for breakfast, as a snack food on the trail, or as ingredients in desserts.
- **Couscous.** Couscous is available in two types: the whole wheat version, which is less processed and a light brown color, or the more refined and traditional version, which is yellow. Both types cook fast and can be hydrated and eaten right out of your camp cup. Couscous can be mixed with sweetener, dried fruits, and nuts for a hot breakfast (or combined with cheese and veggies for a tasty dinner).
- **Hash-brown potatoes.** Dried, shredded, or scalloped, hash browns make an excellent breakfast (or dinner). They are best served

in fried form with cheese and seasonings, or with bacon or sausage for a hearty meal.

- **Pancakes.** Use a quick, add-water-only commercial brand to whip up a batch of hotcakes for breakfast.
- **Bagels, muffins, and English muffins.** Many bread products are available commercially and are, of course, very versatile for either breakfast, lunch, or dinner.
- **Powdered eggs.** Powdered eggs are a great substitute for real eggs for breakfast favorites such as scrambled eggs, omelets, or French toast.

## Dinner Daydreams

- **Pasta.** Pastas, made from white and whole grain flours, come in a wide variety of shapes and colors. Pasta is a popular dinner food that can be used in many recipes from soups to main dishes.
- **Instant beans.** Pinto and black beans are available dried or refried in most grocery stores or natural food shops. Beans are great with tortillas or rice or in combination

with pasta. Leftovers make good dips or spreads with crackers or tortillas.

- **Instant lentils.** Lentils are good with rice, in soups, or to make vegetarian burgers. They are available in most natural food stores.
- **Falafel.** Instant falafel can be mixed with water, formed into patties, and fried as a veggie burger served with rice or bread. It is very spicy!
- **Instant barley.** Quick-cooking barley is a good ingredient in soups or mixed with various grains for a main meal.
- **Hummus.** Hummus makes an excellent dip or spread with crackers or pita bread.
- **Bulgur.** Bulgur is nice in soups or mixed with other grains. Bulgur is the main ingredient in tabouli, a popular cold Lebanese salad (see the *Recipes* section). It can be used in many ways, including served hot for breakfast.
- **Instant potato pearls or flakes.** Instant potatoes make a good thickener for soups and gravies. They are also excellent served alone or as an addition to a main meal.

Cooked with cheese, margarine, and a cup-of-soup packet, instant potatoes make a quick mini-meal. They can also be used for a savory breakfast or mixed with flour to make potato pancakes. **Note:** Potato pearls are preseasoned; potato flakes are bland, and you will want milk, butter, etc. to get them to taste good.

- **Rice: white, brown, pilaf, basmati.** Rice, available in many varieties, is a versatile mainstay. Instant rice cooks the fastest and mixes well with lentils or beans. It can also be sweetened and served for breakfast.
- **Tortillas, pita breads, flat breads, baguette.** These bread products are great additions to main meals (or as ready-to-eat snacks for the trail). However, they can be bulky and are perishable.
- **Soups.** Cup-of-soups can be sipped or added to potato pearls with cheese for a quick meal. Ramen soups mix well with canned meats and cheese. Soup bases, including bouillon cubes or broth packets (chicken, beef, veggie, miso), are good for

seasoning and can
be sipped when all
other soups are
gone.

- **Sauces.** Tomato base
  is a complete tomato
  product in powdered
  form (just add water).
  Packaged sauce and
  seasoning mixes such
  as white, cheese,
  spaghetti, chili, pesto,
  and alfredo are also
  great to use with pasta.
- **Dried and fresh vegetables.** Dried
  veggies are an excellent way to add color
  and texture to colorless entrees. Mixed
  vegetables, green and red bell peppers,
  peas, and carrots are all used at NOLS. Fresh
  vegetables are also a nice option on short
  trips. However, don't add freshies to your
  overall calculated food weight, as their
  sustenance to weight ratio will throw off
  your total. A half-pound onion will not give

you the same nourishment as a half-pound
of summer sausage, for example.

- **Meat: jerky, sliced pepperoni, cooked
bacon bits, sausage crumbles.** These
precooked, flavorful options are all
especially good for winter trips because
they can withstand freeze-thaw conditions
and provide much needed protein.
- **Meat substitutes: tempeh, nut butters,
textured vegetable protein.** Textured vegetable protein, made from soybeans, can be
mixed with other ingredients to make a
veggie burger or chili mix. It is a good
source of protein for vegetarians.
- **Dessert mixes.** The easiest option is to
buy dessert mixes that require only water.
Options include cheesecakes, brownies
(which can be scrambled for quick gratifi-
cation), gingerbread (wonderful added
to pancake mixes), instant puddings, and
gelatin.

### Tasty Trail Treats

- **Nuts.** A great trail food, nuts can be eaten
alone or mixed with dried fruits and candy

to make GORP (what we call trail mix at NOLS; see our recipe on page 96). They may also make a fine addition to main dishes.

- **Seeds: roasted or raw.** Pumpkin, sunflower, sesame, and piñon seeds can be eaten plain or added to GORP. They can be added to breakfast and dinner dishes.
- **Dried and fresh fruits.** Dried fruit options include individual fruits and berries, mixed fruit combinations, and fruit leathers. Like fresh vegetables, fresh fruit is also nice to be able to bring on short trips. But remember, don't add the weight to your projected food needs. You could quickly end up with 3 pounds of fresh fruit, but you don't want that taking away from the

mmmm...

# A Quick Look at Food Ideas

other needed rations that round out a well-balanced meal plan.

- **Cookies and crackers.** With a plethora of types and flavors to choose from, cookies such as Fig Newtons, fruit bars, animal crackers, granola bars, and Pop-Tarts hold up well in a backpack. Crackers are great for dips and spreadables such as cheese, nut butters, and hummus. Choose from flavored and shaped crackers, melba toasts, bagel chips, pretzels, and croutons.

    **Hint:** Pack them in plastic containers with secure lids for protection.

- **Corn nuts and soy nuts.** Corn nuts and soy nuts are salty, crunchy, and cheap, with a strong flavor. But you need to be careful—they can break teeth.

- **Energy bars: store bought or homemade.** The list of choices is long, and they make great pick-me-ups, meal replacements, or meal supplements. Some varieties are wheat-free, gluten-free, and dairy-free.

- **Candy.** Backcountry favorites include candy bars, chocolate- or yogurt-covered nuts and fruits, and wrapped hard candies.

**Hint:** Remove wrappers as you bag them to prevent litter.

## Bountiful Beverages

- **Drink mixes.** Lemonade, Tang, apple cider, Gatorade, Jell-O (makes a great hot drink), presweetened Kool-Aid or Crystal Light (great weight savers) are some of the choices.
- **Tea (bags or instant powder varieties).**
- **Hot chocolate (you can stretch it with powdered milk).**
- **Coffee.** Carry instant—or instant flavored coffee drinks—or carry ground beans and make yourself a thick cup of Cowboy Coffee (see page 74).

## Spicy Thoughts

A spice kit is an important part of any cooking experience. But remember—not everyone has the same taste buds, so proceed with caution.

**Note:** At NOLS we do not count the weight of spices as a part of the overall plan.

## A Quick Look at Food Ideas

- **Basil:** A sweet-smelling leaf that adds a complementary flavor to pasta and potatoes.
- **Black pepper:** Adds a hearty richness to most dishes.
- **Cayenne:** Ground red pepper, and very hot.
- **Cinnamon:** Strong and sweet, great in cereals and hot drinks.
- **Cumin powder:** Brings out the flavor in many dishes, especially beans.
- **Curry powder:** A strong taste, and hot if you use too much. Good in rice and fruit dishes.
- **Dill weed:** Makes a nice addition to soups, especially the creamy ones.

- **Garlic powder:** If you like it, it will boost the flavor of just about any dish.
- **Mustard powder:** Gives a nice kick to pasta and bean dishes.
- **Onion flakes:** A great substitute for fresh onion. One tablespoon equals about one-half a medium onion.
- **Oregano:** Similar to basil, and adds a sweet subtlety to Italian dishes.
- **Salt:** A bland or "soapy" taste is most often due to a lack of salt. Salt brings out the flavor in everything. But, once again, taste first.
- **Spike:** One of the more popular seasoning spices found in natural food stores.
- **Vinegar:** Good as a flavoring, great in sauces; apple cider vinegar, especially, has a nice hearty flavor. Balsamic can be mixed with olive oil as a dip for bread.
- **Tabasco/hot sauce:** Great condiment for grains, pastas, and soups.

## Hard-to-Find Items

The following hard-to-find items are available
through mail-order from NOLS Rocky Mountain
Rations Department, 502 Lincoln Street, Lander,
Wyoming 82520; 307-332-1419:

- Dried vegetables (mixed veggies, green and
  red bell peppers, peas and carrots, onions,
  spinach, broccoli, and jalapeños)
- Shredded dehydrated hash browns
- Potato pearls (seasoned)
- Powdered whole eggs
- Powdered tomato base for sauces and soups
- Chickenish Bits (textured vegetable protein)

### Step 3

*Estimate how much food you will need at each meal
to feed the number of people going on the trip.* At
this point, things can become a bit more com-
plicated. How big are the appetites involved?
How strenuous is the trip? What time of year
are you heading out? At NOLS we approach
the question of "how much" by weight. For
overall poundage, here are some rough guidelines to start you planning:

- 1.0 to 1.5 pounds/person/day (gives you
  roughly 2,500 to 3,000 calories/person/

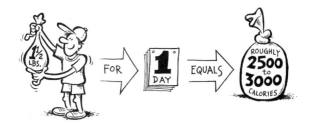

day). This amount works well for short trips when you anticipate hot days and warm nights. It is an excellent amount for trips with children and for leisurely days, especially if you are fishing to supplement your menu.

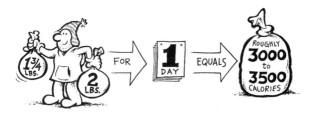

- 1.75 to 2.0 pounds/person/day (gives you roughly 3,000 to 3,500 calories/person/day). This amount works well when you expect warm or cool days and nights or when you anticipate days of moderate to strenuous exercise, such as shouldering a heavy pack over long distances. If the exercise level will be high, better to opt for 2.0 pounds/person/day.

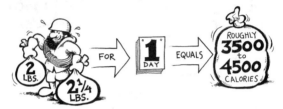

- 2.0 to 2.25 pounds/person/day (gives you roughly 3,500 to 4,500 calories/person/day). Good for heavy workdays and cold temperatures, this amount works well for hiking or skiing with full packs during the cool days and cold nights of early spring, late fall, or winter.

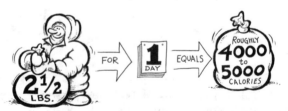

- 2.5 pounds/person/day (gives you roughly 4,000 to 5,000 calories/person/day). This amount is good for cold days and extremely cold nights, such as in mid-winter, when you are skiing with full packs or hauling sleds in mountain environments. At NOLS we seldom pack this much weight, and you probably will not either on a short trip.

For our example, let's say you've invited two friends along for your weekend getaway. The September days will be warm, but the nights will be chilly, and you will be covering a lot of miles—so you will shoot for 1.75 pounds/person/day. Total food weight: 3 people x 2 days x 1.75 pounds = 10.5 pounds.

**Step 4**
*Break down the total poundage into a shopping list based on your menu.* Remember, this is not an exact science, so keep an open mind and don't be afraid to round your numbers. It may seem confusing at first, but you will get the hang of it.

Now, there are two ways to determine food weight so that you're confident in the end that you have packed enough chow. After gathering and repackaging it, you could simply weigh the food with a scale. However, not

## How Many Are Too Many?

If group size grows beyond four people (or five small eaters), you should consider two cook groups—which means two stoves. More than three to four people in a cook group tend to burden a stove with too much pressure. Not only do meals start taking too long to prepare, but the temperament of groups has been well documented to deteriorate.

everyone has a food scale, so the easy fix is to notice the weight of the food listed on all packaged food you buy before repackaging. Say, as an example, you have a box of falafel mix (just add water and fry). The box lists the weight of the product at six ounces. The package says you are getting five servings in the box, or 1.2 ounces per serving. If you want to pack three servings, repackage approximately three-fifths of the product in a small plastic bag. With about three-fifths of the package of falafel, you will have about 3.6 ounces of food.

inexpensive
POSTAL
SCALE

You will also probably be packing some foods in bulk: coffee, sugar for cereal and coffee, powdered milk, powdered drink mix, margarine, cheese, and hot chocolate. You can, of course, buy items such as hot chocolate in individual packets, but they cost more and add to the trash you have to pack out. Bulk items typically fall into that category of foods that can be served at more than one meal. Since you don't need absolute precision, if you have a lot of these bulk items at home, you can determine approximate weight by using the "Weight-by-Cup" section (see page 98), which includes information on the most common items. With all of this in mind, your shopping list for three people for the upcoming weekend trip based on our sample meal plan would be:

FALAFAL MIX 6 oz

3.6 oz

2.4 oz SUBTRACTED

**Necessities**

- **Margarine (1 cup)—9 ounces.** This weight is from the "Weight-by-Cup" section. A half cup will be enough to make fried rice, fry the bagels for breakfast, and make the no-bake cookies.
- **Powdered milk—3 ounces.** You think less than a cup will do, and a cup weighs $3\frac{1}{3}$ ounces. You will mix it with cold water to add to the granola with a little left over to whiten the coffee.
- **Cheese—16 ounces total;** 8 ounces of pepper jack and 8 ounces of havarti. A pound of cheese looks about right for 1 breakfast and 1 lunch, with a little left over to add to your Gado-Gado or to snack on.
- **Sugar (brown, 1 cup)—6 ounces.** This weight is from the "Weight-by-Cup" list. You might like sugar in your coffee, you might want to add a spoonful to your granola, and you will need some for the no-bake cookies.

**Total Necessities Weight: 34 ounces (2.1 pounds)**

**Breakfast**

- **Granola—15 ounces.** Based on your breakfast needs for the first morning, the package says 3 servings weigh 15 ounces.
- **Bagels (3)—9 ounces.** The package says 3 bagels weigh 9 ounces, one each for breakfast.
- **Summer sausage—8 ounces.** A 1-pound summer sausage looks like it will be enough for trail food and as a topping for fried bagels at breakfast. We'll calculate half that pound here.

**Total Breakfast Weight: 32 ounces (2 pounds)**

**Dinner**

- **Instant soup (3 packets)—3.5 ounces.** You want 3 cups of soup, and the individual packets weigh 1.15 ounces each.
- **Noodles—8 ounces.** The NOLS Gado-Gado Spaghetti recipe (page 78) calls for ½ pound (8 ounces) of noodles.
- **Fruit bars—12 ounces.** You decide you want a dozen, four for each person on the trip, and they weigh about an ounce each.
- **Rice (2 cups)—15 ounces.** You need 2 cups for Fried Rice for three people; the weight is from the "Weight-by-Cup" section on page 98.

- **Oatmeal (1 cup)—2.75 ounces.** This is for the No-Bake Eskimo Cookies for dinner your second night and snacks (recipe page 96.)

**Total Dinner Weight: 41.25 ounces (2.6 pounds)**

**Trail Food**
- **Peanut butter (1 cup)—9 ounces.** You figure a cup will provide enough spread for crackers at one lunch for three people since you will also be having trail mix, etc.
- **Crackers—6 ounces.** The package says one serving weighs 2 ounces, and you think, with the other trail food, one serving each will be enough.
- **Summer sausage—8 ounces.** A 1-pound summer sausage looks like it will be enough for trail food and as a topping for fried bagels at breakfast. We'll calculate half that pound here.
- **Bagels (3)—9 ounces.** The package says 3 bagels, one each for trail food, weigh 9 ounces.
- **GORP—16 ounces.** One pound of your mixture of peanuts, M&Ms, and raisins will be enough for two lunches.

**Total Trail Food Weight: 48 ounces (3 pounds)**

**Beverages**
- **Hot chocolate (2 cups)—9 ounces.** This should be enough for hot chocolate for two dinners plus about 3 tablespoons for the no-bake cookies.
- **Coffee (ground, 12 tablespoons)—3 ounces.** This weight is from the "Weight-by-Cup" section and is enough to make 6 cups of Cowboy Coffee (page 74) for two mornings.
- **Drink mix—2 ounces.** A 2-ounce packet of drink mix should make enough for the trail.

**Total Beverage Weight: 14 ounces (0.9 pounds)**

**Spices**
You will package the spices and small amounts of additional ingredients for the recipes according to the meal-in-a-bag plan, and you will not count these additions as a part of the total weight.

**Total Menu Weight: 10.6 pounds**

**Step 5**

*Go shopping for the grub.* "Shopping" does not mean you actually have to make a trip to the local market. Most people, we figure, can find enough food for a weekend trip by searching through their own kitchen at home. Check the fridge for cheese, margarine, and tortillas. Look through the cupboard for instant potatoes and instant rice, boxes of macaroni and cheese, jerky, candy, nuts, seeds, crackers, peanut butter, dried fruit, pita bread, brown sugar, honey, hot chocolate, tea bags, and coffee. Include in your search the corners of the pantry where individual packets of instant oatmeal, boxes of falafel, and bags of granola hide with expiration dates that have not yet arrived.

You can supplement the pantry raid with a visit to your favorite grocery store. A quick trip and you can walk out with instant Cream of

Wheat and rice cereal. Throw in some butter, nuts, and/or dried fruit to extend the staying power (and taste) of cereals. Buy some powdered milk for hot drinks such as tea and coffee.

**Step 6**

*Repackage and pack your food for the trip.* With the trip's food purchased and assembled, you are ready to repackage everything. This is, of course, not absolutely required on a shorter journey, but we strongly recommend it. Cardboard, paper, foil, and cans are all excess weight and potential litter.

At NOLS, we use two-ply clear plastic bags to package almost all food. We purchase commercial bags that can be lightly tied in a

EXCESS PACKAGING

ZIP LOCK

knot, "lightly" being an important concept to master. Contrary to the beliefs of the uninitiated, food will not spill out of a bag tied with a loose knot. Food will not spill with a tight knot either, but untying tight knots in plastic may take longer than cooking dinner. Plastic bags are lightweight and reusable and allow you to see inside. Most of the food will be easily identifiable via sight, smell, or a quick taste, but, if you are worried, use a permanent marker to identify the contents.

And do not worry if you fail to find commercial bags. You can use zip-top plastic bags, freezer bags, Seal-a-Meal bags, Tupperware, and squeeze tubes.

Nalgene bottle

old plastic peanut butter jar

Ziploc tub

Rubbermaid tub

To save the maximum amount of time and searching, use the meal-in-a-bag plan: Carry all the ingredients for a specific meal in one large plastic bag. If all the ingredients are not cooked at the same time, you will have to use smaller bags to separate the ingredients within the large bag. Pasta for four, as an example, can go into a large bag. Within the bag of pasta, you can pack smaller bags containing smoked salmon, vegetables, and seasoning to add to the pasta after it has cooked and been drained. Voila! A meal-in-a-bag.

With the meal planning system, you may want to package each day's meals together or pack breakfasts and dinners together by meal type. Lunch items (trail food) can be packed all together in a larger bag, ready to pull out and munch on when hunger strikes. Label with a permanent marker (Example: Dinner, Day One) and include recipe instructions.

ploc Bag

tiny Ziploc baggie

Squeeze tube

Simple clip for closure

## Sample Meal-in-a-Bag

**SMOKED SALMON PASTA (SERVES 4)**

- 4 garlic cloves
- 2 green onions
- 3 Tbs. margarine
- 4 Tbs. dried tomato bits
- 1 packet instant chicken broth
- $\frac{1}{2}$ cup water
- 8 oz. smoked salmon
- 8 oz. angel hair pasta
- $\frac{1}{4}$ cup capers
- Parmesan cheese

Peel and chop garlic and green onions, and sauté in margarine. Add dried tomato bits, chicken broth, and $\frac{1}{2}$ cup water. Let sit off heat for 15–20 minutes while pasta cooks. Flake salmon into garlic-tomato mix, and add capers. Drain pasta.

Toss pasta and salmon-garlic-tomato mix until well mixed. Serve sprinkled with Parmesan cheese.

Let's see what we can do at home before we leave so everything is ready for an easy, yet deliciously creative, dinner once we're in the backcountry.

- Pack the pasta in a large plastic bag.
- Peel and chop garlic and onions and place in a small plastic bag.
- Put broth packet and tomato bits into a small plastic bag.
- Flake salmon into a small plastic bag, and put in capers.
- Package some Parmesan cheese in a small plastic bag.
- Put all the small plastic bags in the large bag with the pasta.
- Pack margarine separately in a small container in bulk, ready for this and other uses.

# Packing Tips

- Have each person carry their share of the food and kitchen equipment in a small, zippered, nylon duffel. Yes, the duffel adds a smidgeon of weight, but the convenience outweighs the ounces of the bag.

FOOD:
It's heavy,
So pack it high
(above)

↓

POSSIBLE
CONTAMINANTS!

- Always be careful when packing food to avoid any chance of contamination by soap, stove fuel, or a leaky lighter. Try to keep the food above these items in your pack.

- Backpackers, generally, should carry heavy items such as food high and close to the body, unless they will be hiking through boulder fields or deadfall. In these conditions, carry most of the weight lower, for better balance when jumping or twisting.

ON TRAIL HIKING

OFF TRAIL HIKING

# Cook to
# PERFECTION

In addition to food and recipes, cooking creatively in the field will require not only a few tools (stove, pots, pans, etc.) but also the skill to use them appropriately. This section covers the tools and the basic skills.

# Stoves

**W**ithout a trustworthy source of heat with enough intensity for cooking, you will not be cooking—backcountry or otherwise. Although nothing inherently evil dwells in the flames of a campfire, fires may be forbidden and/or environmentally unacceptable in your area of travel—both great reasons to not build one. Cooking, or attempting to cook, on an acceptable fire creates many possibilities for learning and burning, but the skill of campfire cooking asks more than the scope of this book. We will therefore discuss stoves. Numerous excellent backpacking stoves are available today. If you do not already own a stove, and even if you do, here are some thoughts on choosing a reliable one:

- **Size and weight:** A good stove packs neatly and easily, and it weighs, ideally, no more than a pound without fuel.
- **Heat generated:** A good stove will boil a liter of water in a few minutes when set on high heat, but it will also be capable of low heat for simmering.
- **Ease of use:** A good stove is easy to fire up and operate.
- **Stability:** A good stove has a base wide and strong enough to prevent dinner from ending up in the dirt.
- **Toughness:** A good stove can take a beating and keep on cooking.
- **Fuel type:** A good stove burns a readily available and efficient type of fuel. With those two guidelines in mind, we prefer stoves that burn white gas. White gas stoves require you to carry fuel in a separate container from which you periodically refill the stove's tank. Some great stoves utilize butane or propane, or a butane/propane mix—fuel that must be carried in cartridges. Stoves utilizing fuel in cartridges are easier to use than white gas stoves, but the fuel is more expensive.

# Figuring Fuel

**Summer:** Figure about one-sixth liter per person per day, or about one-third liter per stove per day for a three-person cook group.

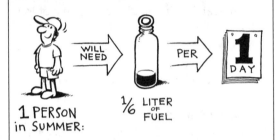

1 PERSON in SUMMER:

WILL NEED

⅙ LITER OF FUEL

PER

1 DAY

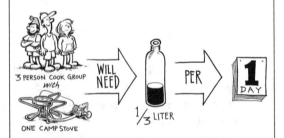

3 PERSON COOK GROUP with ONE CAMP STOVE

WILL NEED

⅓ LITER

PER

1 DAY

**Spring/Fall:** Figure about one-fourth liter per person per day (assuming you will want more hot drinks), or one-half liter per stove per day for a three-person cook group.

**Winter:** Figure about one-half liter per person per day (especially if you will be melting snow for water), or three-fourths liter per stove per day for a three-person cook group.

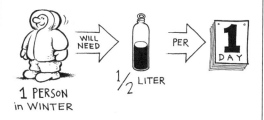

1 PERSON in WINTER — WILL NEED — $\frac{1}{2}$ LITER — PER — 1 DAY

3 PERSON COOK GROUP with ONE CAMP STOVE — WILL NEED — $\frac{3}{4}$ LITER — PER — 1 DAY

And, yes, these are estimates, and variables, such as type of stove and fuel, are certain. But you will almost always be safe with these numbers.

## TIPS FOR STOVE USE, SAFETY, AND MAINTENANCE

- Be sure to practice using your stove and repairing your stove before you leave home.
- Carry a repair kit for your stove.
- When cooking, place your stove on a level surface protected from the wind and away from any vegetation. Keep the area clear of all burnable materials. Keep water handy in case material you overlooked ignites. Watch out for sand and dirt that can clog the valves or fuel line. If you are traveling in an area where it is impossible to get out of the sand or where you will be in snow, consider taking a stove pad or a piece of fire cloth to cook on. Position the stove with the on-off valve accessible.
- Store fuel in bottles made for fuel storage. Use funnels or pouring spouts to fill your stove. Fill stoves away from your cooking area and any open flames. Fill stoves no more than three-fourths full so you have space for pressure. Do not fill a stove with fuel when the stove is hot.
- If fuel spills on the stove, allow it to evaporate before lighting.

- Fill your stove after every meal. If you have an emergency, your stove will always be ready.
- Keep stoves covered when not in use. Carry stoves in a stuff sack or kit. These tips prolong a stove's life and reduce maintenance by keeping dust and dirt out.
- Because of the potential for flare-ups and carbon monoxide poisoning, we do not recommend using stoves inside a tent.
- If you have to cook under a tarp or tent vestibule, at least fill and light your stove somewhere far away. Nylon melts easily and quickly. Keep the area in which you are cooking well-ventilated.
- Pack several matchbooks (and a lighter) in different places, and place them in individual plastic bags to keep them dry and ready to provide ignition for your stove.

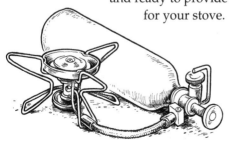

# Kitchen
# EQUIPMENT

With a stove hissing appropriately, you only need a minimum of kitchen gear to cook and eat well. Depending on the size of the group, the menu, and the type of activity (paddling a canoe, for instance, gives you the opportunity to carry more weighty and varied kitchen equipment), you will want one or two 2- to 4-liter pots. If you carry two, be sure they nest together to save space. We prefer stainless steel, but aluminum is lighter and less expensive. Titanium works great if you can afford it. Frying produces delicious food and requires one nonstick 10- or 12-inch fry pan with a lid and no plastic parts. We also recommend one large spoon, one spatula, one collapsible 1.5- to 2.5-gallon water jug or

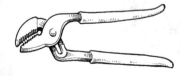 

water bag, and a pair of pliers or potgrips. And we carry a 4-inch metal strainer to remove food particles from waste-water (see the "Environmental Considerations" chapter for more information). On an individual level, everyone will want a spoon and a mug (usually an insulated 12- to 20-ounce cup with a snug-fitting lid). We also prefer everyone to have a small bowl (which can be no more than a disposable storage tub from the grocery store). Since everyone will have at least one personal water bottle, choosing one with graduations for measurement eliminates the need for a measuring cup.

PLASTIC SPOON
with a
cut off handle
(one per person)

LID

plastic
BOWL

ROCK
(available at each)
campsite

old aluminium
PIE PLATE

tiny
POT
GRABBERS

Simple
COOK POT

**No MUG!**
drink your hot tea
out of
your water bottle

# lightweight COOK SYSTEM
(carried on your back)

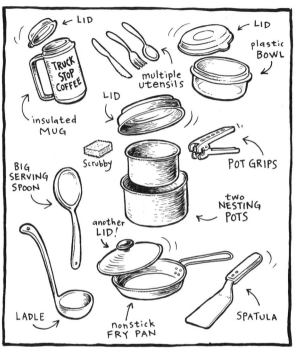

# heavyweight COOK SYSTEM
(when it's NOT on your back, like on a canoe)

# Cooking
## BASICS

**A**nybody can ruin what could have been a fine meal with, say, too much heat or too much chili powder. Conversely, anybody, with attention to a few details, can prepare a delicious and completely satisfying repast.

### JUST SAY NO TO BURNED FOOD
Thoreau suggested embracing simplicity—and here's the simplest way to prevent burned food: Do not leave the kitchen during meal prep. Lightweight cook pots are typically thin on the bottom and transmit heat rapidly. Two minutes on high heat is all it takes to create a partially blackened ruin. No matter how much you season a pot of burned rice, it still tastes like burned rice.

Always start with a clean pot to avoid burning old food stuck on the bottom. A general rule is to bring the water to a boil, add the contents, and stir. Then turn the heat to low, cover, and simmer, checking frequently by sticking a clean spoon down the middle of the contents to see the bottom of the pot. If you wait to smell something burning, you have almost always waited too long.

Use too much rather than too little water. A too-soupy dinner remains edible and most often tasty. A burned dinner is neither. Remember: You can add water after the cooking has started if the pot looks like it needs it. You can also add water to a frying pan to prevent burning. If the goal of frying is a crispy dish, added water may reduce crispiness—but soggy beats burned.

Eggs, cheese, and milk are especially easy to burn. Butter burns easily; margarine and oil less so. Watch these foods carefully. Add ingredients such as dried milk, cheese, or potato pearls just before a dish is done to avoid scorching.

Overcooked—but short of burned—food results most often from poor estimation of the different cooking times of different ingredients. As an example of good timing: Add freeze-dried food to cold water, boil 8–10 minutes, and then add rice or pasta.

## Saving the Soupy

If your meal sloshes around soupily (too much water) after being cooked, you are not necessarily stuck with it that way. You may use any of the following ingredients to thicken your food: flour, potato flakes, a dried egg-and-milk powder mix, or even instant cereals. To prevent clumps of the ingredient used to thicken a watery meal, mix the ingredient with a little water to form a paste, and then add the paste to the pot.

## SPICING UP YOUR LIFE

As we mentioned in chapter 1, a thoughtfully planned, lightweight spice kit will add flavor and edibility to every meal. Seasoning a meal is, however, an art that requires practice, and, like beauty, is ultimately a matter of personal taste. Your companions may prefer to add spices to their portions instead of suffering with your decisions. Here are some guidelines:

- You will not need an entire container of oregano. Repackage spices in little containers—many small sizes are commercially available. Or repackage your spices in little plastic bags, like the ones you find in jewelry or bead stores, thinking small and taking only enough for the upcoming trip.

- Do not add spices directly from a container. One spill, and the anticipated meal may end up inedible. Pour spices into a spoon or container lid, then add them to a dish. Your hands, for potentially unhygienic reasons, are unacceptable tools.
- Do not assume a dish needs a certain spice, and especially do not add salt to commercially packaged foods. They may be too salty right out of the bag. Taste them before deciding.
- The flavor of many spices intensifies as they cook. Add a little spice, allow a few minutes of cooking time, and taste to decide if you want to add more.

## MINIMIZING COOKING TIME/MAXIMIZING FUEL USED

Proper planning prevents poor performance. Have the kitchen set up and everything ready at hand before firing up the stove for dinner. The one-burner does not need to hiss furiously, uselessly burning white gas, while you run down to the creek for a pot of water. Choose a sheltered spot for the stove and use a wind shield or windscreen, especially if the wind is blowing. Even on a still day, a windscreen helps concentrate the heat under a pot or pan. Many stoves come with a windscreen, or you can purchase them separately.

Cook with a cover on pots to reduce cooking time and, therefore, the amount of fuel used. Lift the cover no more than necessary since each lift allows heat to escape, reducing stove efficiency and increasing the cooking time. You will need to check cooking food frequently, but you do not need to check water to see if it is boiling. Boiling will send steam from under the cover.

KEEP FUEL AWAY
from the stove
and food!

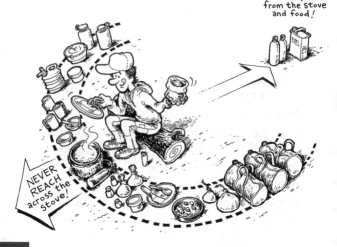

NEVER REACH across the stove!

## Cooking Safety Tips

- Do not pour hot water into handheld containers. Burns are one of the leading causes of backcountry evacuations.
- Do not use your leg or any other part of your body as a cutting board. When using a knife, cut away from yourself.
- Do not forget to wash your hands prior to food prep. Illnesses from germs are more common than injuries in backcountry kitchens.

Presoaking dehydrated vegetables and beans throughout the day can save time. A water bottle works well for this. Do not, by the way, presoak pasta—it will turn to mush.

# **Environmental**
# CONSIDERATIONS

**T**wo things should never happen in the backcountry kitchen:

1. No one should walk away without ingesting enough tasty, nourishing grub, and
2. No sign should be left of food preparation and consumption.

"Leave no trace" rings forth, quietly but determinedly, as the mantra of the ethically motivated backcountry user, and no place in camp offers as much chance to leave long-lasting impact as the kitchen. Litter, to say the least, then fire scars, compacted soil and vegetation, and habituated animals are all indicators of unnecessary human disturbance of wild lands.

Leaving no trace in the backcountry kitchen starts at home. Plan ahead and prepare by repackaging food in lightweight plastic bags to minimize potential litter (and to

## Leave No Trace

Guidelines for minimizing the social and environmental impact of backcountry visitors have been developed by the national Leave No Trace education program. These guidelines are summarized as the following Leave No Trace principles:

1. Plan ahead and prepare.
2. Camp and travel on durable surfaces.
3. Dispose of waste properly.
4. Leave what you find.
5. Minimize campfire impacts.
6. Respect wildlife.
7. Be considerate of other visitors.

For more information and written materials, call the Leave No Trace office at 1-800-332-4100, or visit their Web site at www.lnt.org.

lighten your load). In addition to the black and everlasting scar left from a fire, the greatest impact of a kitchen, and to the backcountry in general, comes from compaction of the soil and destruction of vegetation. According to the U.S. Forest Service, a campsite utilized more than ten times does not significantly deteriorate with further use. Most of the impact, in fact, comes with the first one or two times a site is used improperly. So if you have a choice between an obviously impacted spot and a nearby pristine spot, use the heavily impacted spot and you will do less damage.

When you do camp in an unspoiled area, choosing the cooking site ranks as the single most important consideration. Start looking for the best site early, before fatigue or darkness urges you to drop down in the most convenient space. If you see evidence of previous light use, go somewhere else. Ideal spots are without vegetation, or even soil. Look for sand, rocks, gravel, or snow. Second best are soil-based sites without vegetation where your stay will cause some compaction but recovery is rapid. When faced with a choice between dense vegetation and sparse vegetation, choose dense. Sparse plant life is destroyed easier than a thick carpet of vegetation. Stay off marshy ground, wet grass, dewy flowers, low shrubs, and baby trees—they all take a long time to come back from abuse. Dense dry grass, on the other hand, makes a tough durable surface. A camp in an open meadow of grass (even though possibly more visible to other campers) recovers more quickly than thin vegetation hidden under a forest canopy. In summary, find a place on the earth that works—do not rearrange the earth to create a place.

Larger groups (more than four or five) leave less impact, especially in more pristine areas, if they break up into smaller cook groups. Pack in and wear soft-soled shoes instead of boots in and around the kitchen to reduce stress on the land. Reduce your movement around the kitchen as much as possible, especially in vegetated spots. Avoid making trails. Walking back and forth from tent to stove along the same path several times may leave a track noticeable for years. Minimize your stay in one place. Less trace is left on the land if you move camp every day.

With proper meal planning and careful cooking, you can eliminate most leftovers. If you do end up with extra cooked food, eat it later—if it can be kept cool enough and reheated—or carry it out. Do not bury food scraps or use a fire to dispose of food (or nonburnable trash such as Styrofoam or aluminum). Food scraps, like other trash, have

no place in the backcountry. Pack out what you packed in.

Certain waste—including wastewater from cooking and washing—cannot be packed out, practically speaking. Scatter wastewater widely, at least 200 feet away from any water source and far away from campsites. Before scattering cooking water, remove all food particles (a small strainer is good for this) and pack them out with your trash. Fish guts are an exception. In some parts of Wyoming, for instance, the recommended procedure is to toss fish parts back into the same water source from which they came. Be sure to toss the viscera into deep (and, if possible, moving) water to help scatter the parts. For other areas of the country, check with local game and fish management experts for recommendations.

At NOLS, we use soap only for washing hands before food preparation. We clean kitchen gear with nature's scrub brushes—sand, pinecones, pine needles, bunches of grass or snow—and give them a rinse with boiling water just prior to eating. With this method, no soapy dishwater is added to the environment, and it helps prevent stomach upsets caused by soap residue on the dishes. However, if you want to use soap, carry a small bottle of biodegradable soap. Do your dishes at least 200 feet away from any water source to prevent environmental contamination. Remember, even biodegradable soap is a foreign chemical in aquatic environments and should be used sparingly—a few drops will do.

When you are packed and ready to move on, check one more time to make sure you are leaving no trace. Look for spillage at the cooking site, flour or rice that puffed out of the pot during mixing, food that fell off the plate while eating in the dark. Fluff up grass or other vegetation that got pressed down. Sprinkle duff or other natural materials over marred areas.

Replace rocks or logs you may have rolled out of the way. Use a dead branch to sweep away even your tracks.

**WATER DISINFECTION**

Drinking enough water is more important to you than eating enough food. The old adage saying you should drink enough water to keep your urine output clear and copious is essentially true. But no matter how remote the source, or pristine its appearance, water may contain microorganisms that cause illness. So disinfect water by boiling, chemical treatment with iodine or chlorine, or filtration.

Incorrect information persists on how long to boil water before it is disinfected. Common pathogens (disease-causing microorganisms) die immediately in boiling water. By the time water boils, in other words, it is safe to drink. The boiling point decreases with increasing elevation, but this does not affect disinfection. The boiling point at 19,000 feet is 178°F (81°C), which is sufficient for disinfecting water. Pathogens are also killed in the cooking process, so you do not need to use treated water in pots and pans that will be heated enough to cook food. For drinking water, most people either use a filter or treat their water with chemicals. In both cases, you need to read the labels to make sure the disinfection method does what you want it to do, and that you are using the method correctly.

**EXTREMES OF COLD**

Neither stoves—nor people—function at their very best in extremes of cold. Some stoves will require preheating in order to work. Some stoves will not work at all in deep cold, especially those with fuel in a cartridge. Be sure to understand your stove's capabilities. Camp early. Cold adds enough stress without the further addition of darkness. Start by creating a sheltered area for your kitchen, a concern more important in extremes of cold than any other season. In snow, stamp out or dig out a kitchen area. Get water boiling right away for hot drinks. Wipe the snow off the pots before placing them on the stove. Water dripping on the burner often causes heat inconsistencies. Wear a light pair of gloves while cooking. You will avoid fuel spills on skin and touching metal with a temperature well below freezing—both can cause rapid cold injury. Melting snow for water will take 15–20 minutes, and then you still have to wait for the water to boil. Choose, therefore, meals that require less cooking time. And remember: You can scorch, easily in fact, a snow-filled pot. To avoid scorching, add a little water to the bottom of the pot before adding snow. Remember, also, the additional fuel you will need to melt snow (see "Figuring Fuel" on page 40–41).

**Hint:** Since foods such as cheese, energy bars, salami, and bacon may freeze to the consistency of granite in cold weather, save more time, and frustration, by cutting them into bite-sized pieces before you leave home.

## EXTREMES OF ALTITUDE

As altitude increases, air pressure decreases, and that means both you and your stove will have less oxygen available for functioning. You will eventually acclimatize, but your stove will not. The efficiency of your stove will decrease and stay decreased. It will also take longer for water to boil, and, therefore, it will take longer to cook. As in extremes of cold, you will use more fuel. Once again, simple meals with shorter cooking times are recommended. Carbohydrates are generally more appealing and more easily digested than proteins or fats at high altitudes. Lighter meals are encouraged during the first three days of acclimatization, and small frequent feedings should continue for the entire time at altitude.

## BEARS

Bears have to eat, but they do not have to eat your food or, much worse, you. When traveling in bear country, be sure to check recommended bear practices for the area. Take extra precautions in the selection of your kitchen site. The cooking area should be at least 100 yards from the sleeping area. Be sure to empty

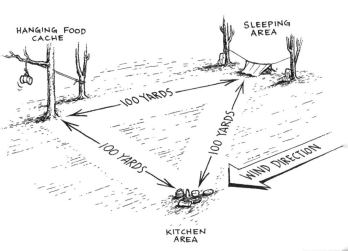

your pack of all food and odorous substances, including trail food, soap, and toothpaste, and store them in the kitchen area. Be extra careful to avoid spills on your clothing. Fish and other greasy food smells are especially attractive to bears, so take precautions to minimize personal contact with these substances. At night, all food and other odorous substances should be protected from bears. If you are camping at tree level, hang food at least 12 feet above the ground at its lowest point and at least 4 feet from any part of the tree. Choose a location at least 100 yards from your sleeping area.

We encourage the use of bear-proof canisters not just above the tree line but anywhere in bear country. Hanging food can be difficult and time-consuming, and a potential safety issue if climbing trees is involved.

# RECIPES

Throughout this chapter are some of NOLS' recipe favorites with tips, hints, recommendations, suggestions, and guidelines that will move you along the trail toward creatively planning an enticing backcountry menu. Remember to look at each with an eye toward preparing and planning as much as you can ahead of time.

# Breakfast
## RECIPES

**B**reakfast is the most important meal of the day. You can eat typical morning fare and walk away having met the standard. But you can also try some never-before-imagined recipes—and create some of your own.

Take hot cereal as an example. You can cook it and eat, or you can cook it and add margarine, milk, sugar, fruit, nuts, cocoa, chocolate chips, or peanut butter in any combination before digging in.

## BREAKFAST COUSCOUS (SERVES 4–5)

This works well as a meal-in-a-bag!

    4 cups water
    1/4 tsp. salt
    3 Tbs. brown sugar or honey
       (check your pantry)
    1/4 cup margarine
    1/4 cup dried fruit (chopped at home)

PREP at HOME

2 cups couscous
2 Tbs. powdered milk mixed with 4 Tbs. water
$\frac{1}{2}$ to 1 tsp. cinnamon
$\frac{1}{4}$ cup sunflower seeds or nuts

Bring water to a boil with salt, brown sugar, margarine, and fruit. Add couscous and milk mixture and stir. Cover and simmer for 5–10 minutes, stirring occasionally. When water is gone and mixture has fluffed up, mix in the cinnamon and nuts.

*Variation:* For Breakfast Bulgur, substitute 2 cups water and 1 cup bulgur for couscous and water; reduce sugar and margarine to 2 Tbs. each; use $\frac{1}{2}$ tsp. either cinnamon or nutmeg. Optional: Stir in 1 tsp. vanilla and 2 Tbs. peanut butter when done.

**Hint:** A 16-ounce (500 ml) plastic Rubbermaid-type storage container with a secure lid makes a great eating bowl and an excellent cooking tool. Add dry ingredients like oatmeal, rice, or couscous to the container, add the recommended amount of boiling water, and quickly add the lid. Wait a few moments, and then shake vigorously! If you shake too soon, the lid will leak because of the pressure caused by expanding hot water. Next, insulate the tub so the meal can cook completely without cooling too soon. Wrap the container in a jacket or stuff it in next to your body. Ready to eat in about 10 minutes. Cleanup is easy: Add warm water, replace the lid, and shake.

## HASH BROWNS WITH CHEESE (SERVES 2–3)

1 ½ cups hash browns
hot water
4 to 5 Tbs. margarine
1 Tbs. onion, rehydrated or fresh
  (nice addition, not required—chop
  it at home)

PREP at HOME

½ cup cheese cubes or grated cheese
  (do the grating at home, or purchase grated
  cheese)
salt and pepper to taste

Put hash browns into a saucepan. Cover with 1 inch of hot water and rehydrate for 15 minutes. Drain off excess water. Melt margarine in a hot fry pan. Add hash browns and onions. Cook, flipping occasionally, until crisp and browned. Stir in or cover with cheese and remove from heat. Cover and allow to sit until cheese is melted. Salt and pepper to taste.

*Variations:* Add ham or bacon bits to hash browns and cook as above. Good with hot sauce or picante.

## DONNA'S HASH BROWN FRITTERS (MAKES EIGHT 3-INCH CAKES)

Makes a great meal-in-a-bag! Powdered milk, flour, egg, pepper, and salt can go in one bag.

    1 cup hash browns
    1 to 2 tsp. dried onion
    hot water
    3 heaping Tbs. powdered milk
    2 Tbs. flour (look in your cupboard)
    3 Tbs. powdered egg
    dash of pepper
    1 tsp. salt

Put hash browns and dried onions into a bowl. Cover with about 1 inch of hot water and rehydrate for 15 minutes. They should be a little firm. In another bowl, stir together dry ingredients. Drain water from potatoes, save it, and add 6 Tbs. of potato water gradually to dry mixture, mixing well. Add this mixture to the potatoes. Drop by large spoonfuls into greased, heated frying pan. Flatten each cake. Cook about 3 minutes on each side until golden brown. Serve with syrup, stewed fruit, or cheese and hot sauce.

## PANCAKES (SERVES 4–5)

Prepare the baking mix before leaving home and pack it along in a plastic bag.

*Baking mix:*

    4 cups flour
    2 ½ Tbs. baking powder
    ¼ cup powdered milk
    2 tsp. salt

*In camp:*

    2 parts baking mix
    1 part flour or uncooked cereal
    enough cold water for a pourable batter

Stir baking mix and flour or dry cereal together. Add cold water gradually until batter is a pourable consistency (not too thick, not too thin). Lightly grease a frying pan and heat until a few drops of water dropped in the hot pan "skitter" on the surface. Pour or spoon batter into pan and cook gently over medium heat until the bubbles on the top surface set. Flip and cook other side. Serve with margarine, peanut butter–honey spread, brown sugar–margarine syrup, or stewed fruit.

*Variations:*

- Add chopped fruit or nuts, raisins, or chocolate or carob chips to batter before cooking.

- Try fruit-flavored Jell-O syrup over your pancakes. Combine 1 cup water, 2 Tbs. brown sugar, 3 Tbs. margarine, and ¼ cup fruit Jell-O mix in pot. Bring to a boil and stir. Let sit for only a short time and pour over cakes.
- For gingerbread pancakes, substitute ½ cup gingerbread mix for 1 cup baking mix. Add 1 tsp. oil or melted margarine to the mix after adding the water.

**Hint:** When using baking powder, never add hot or warm water. It will release its carbon dioxide, and you will end up with flat pancakes.

## HOT SWEET RICE (SERVES 1)

½ cup hot milk
   (2 Tbs. powdered milk in ½ cup water)
½ Tbs. margarine
½ Tbs. brown sugar or honey
dash of cinnamon or nutmeg (you probably
   have some in your kitchen at home)
1 cup cooked rice
2 Tbs. raisins or other fruit and/or nuts

Add the margarine, brown sugar, and cinnamon to hot milk. In a separate bowl, mix fruit and/or nuts into the rice and pour the hot milk mixture over the top. Stir and eat.

## QUICK POTATO CUP (SERVES 1)

2/3 to 3/4 cup hot water
2 to 3 Tbs. powdered milk
1 Tbs. margarine
2/3 cup potato flakes
1/4 cup of cheese in small bits
garlic powder, chili powder, salt and pepper
   to taste

Heat water, milk, and margarine. Stir in potatoes and cheese until just moist. Let stand for 30–60 seconds. Add spices and eat.

## BAGELS

Bagels are a versatile food for breakfast or for a snack. They can be coated with margarine and fried in a pan, or they can be spread with cream cheese, peanut butter, or honey and eaten.
   *Variations:*
• Fried cheese bagels: Fry bagel halves facedown in 2 Tbs. (2 oz.) margarine in a pan. Flip over and layer with 2 oz. cheese. Cover and cook over medium heat for 2–3 minutes. Optional: Sprinkle with hot sauce or spices to taste.

- Bacon bagels: Fry 2 slices bacon and remove from pan. Fry bagel halves facedown in bacon fat. Flip over and layer with 2 oz. cheese. Cover pan and cook for 2–3 minutes until cheese melts. Add crumbled bacon on top. Optional: Add hot sauce or spices to taste.
- Veggie bagels: Add a slice of fresh onion or red or green bell pepper.

# BEVERAGES

**Y**ou can get by fine with water only, but consider a few drinks that will add much pleasure to backcountry dining.

## COWBOY COFFEE (SERVES 4)
    6 cups cold water
    6 Tbs. ground coffee

Bring water to a boil. Add coffee, remove from heat, and cover. Let coffee sit for a couple of minutes. Knock the side of the coffee pot with a spoon or spatula to get the grounds to settle.

**Hint:** A splash of cold water will help make the grounds sink but will not compromise the temperature of the coffee.

## COCOA DELUXE (SERVES 1)

You can mix the dry ingredients in bulk at home and measure 3 Tbs. into 1½ cups hot water on the trail.

**PREP at HOME**

    1½ cups hot water
    2 Tbs. cocoa (hot chocolate) mix
    1 to 2 Tbs. powdered milk
    ½ tsp. vanilla
    dash of cinnamon

Mix cocoa mix and milk into hot water. Add vanilla and cinnamon. Stir.

*Variations:*

- Mocha: Make recipe above, substituting 1½ cups coffee for hot water and adding brown sugar or honey to taste.
- Cocoa Grand Deluxe: Add 1 Tbs. brown sugar and 1 Tbs. margarine for a great winter warmer.
- Super Cocoa: Combine 4 Tbs. cocoa, 2 Tbs. powdered milk, 2 Tbs. brown sugar, and 2 Tbs. peanut butter.

## SUPER TEA (SERVES 4)

6 cups cold water

3 tea bags (Earl Grey, English Breakfast, or other black tea)

3 Tbs. lemon drink mix or 4 Tbs. orange drink mix or apple cider

4 whole cloves or pinch of ground cloves (optional)

pinch of cinnamon and nutmeg (optional)

3 Tbs. honey

Boil water in cooking pot. Add tea bags and steep until desired strength. Stir in fruit drink mix, spices, and honey.

**Hint:** Put some hot water and a tea bag in one of your water bottles at breakfast time. By mid-morning, a cool, refreshing drink will be waiting.

# Dinner
# RECIPES

**A**t the end of the day, with the miles behind you and your campsite established, a major reward of the trail is a fine dinner.

## BASIC PASTA RECIPE (SERVES 2 OR 3)

1 part pasta (2 cups)
2 parts water (4 cups)
salt to taste

Add pasta to boiling, salted water; boil gently 10–15 minutes. Drain water and add your chosen sauce or spices to cooked pasta.

**Note:** When cooking pasta, watch it carefully; it can quickly go from chewy to mushy. Drain it immediately, because leaving it in the water, even if the pan is removed from the heat, continues the cooking process. Adding 1 tsp. of oil or margarine to the cooking water prevents pasta from cementing together when the water is drained.

Rinsing pasta with cool water and straining it with a strainer will reduce the chances of overdone noodles.

*Variations:*

- Add dried veggies to the boiling water.
- Add canned meat to the pasta.
- Leave about ¼ cup water with the noodles and add 3 to 4 Tbs. margarine, 4 Tbs. powdered milk, and 1 cup of diced or grated cheese (grated melts faster) for mac-and-cheese. Pepper and garlic make a nice addition.
- For a change of pace, sauté the mac-and-cheese in a little oil or margarine.

**Hint:** Why waste the water drained from your pasta? Use it for soup or a hot drink.

## DONNA ORR'S GADO-GADO SPAGHETTI (SERVES 2 OR 3)

This will work as a meal-in-a-bag.

½ lb. (2 cups) spaghetti or 2 packages ramen noodles

4 cups water

3 Tbs. + 1 tsp. oil

2 Tbs. sunflower seeds

1 Tbs. dried onion, rehydrated

½ Tbs. or one packet broth

3 Tbs. brown sugar
1 tsp. garlic
1/2 tsp. black pepper (optional)
3/4 cup water, or more as needed
3 Tbs. vinegar
3 Tbs. soy sauce
3 Tbs. peanut butter
sliced green onions (prepare at
    home) or wild onions, if available

PREP at HOME

Break pasta in half and put into boiling
unsalted water to which 1 tsp. of oil has been
added. Cook until done; drain immediately. In a fry
pan, heat 3 Tbs. oil and add the sunflower seeds
and rehydrated onions. Cook and stir over medium
heat for 2 minutes. Add the broth with the brown
sugar, garlic, other spices if desired, and 3/4 cup
water. Add the vinegar and soy sauce. Add peanut
butter and stir. Do not burn! To eat this hot, heat
the sauce thoroughly and pour over hot spaghetti.
Add sliced green or wild onions as a garnish.

**Hint:** This dish can have a fairly salty taste.
Cut back or eliminate the broth if you are con-
cerned about saltiness. The recipe is best cold, and
it loses some of its saltiness as it sits. Mix sauce
and spaghetti, cool quickly, and serve chilled.

## KATIE'S COOL ITALIAN PASTA SALAD
## (SERVES 2 OR 3)

$\frac{1}{2}$ lb. (about 2 cups) pasta

4 cups water

$\frac{1}{2}$ tsp. salt

1 Tbs. dried onion

1 Tbs. dried peppers

1 Tbs. dried mixed veggies

*Dressing (whip this up at home):*

PREP at HOME

1 Tbs. vinegar

$\frac{1}{4}$ cup oil

$\frac{1}{2}$ tsp. garlic powder

2 tsp. Italian seasoning

$\frac{1}{2}$ tsp. salt

pepper to taste

2 Tbs. sunflower seeds

2 Tbs. almonds (broken into pieces)

2 Tbs. dried raisins (cranberries are even
   better!)

Add pasta and vegetables to boiling, salted water and cook for 10–15 minutes. Drain water and combine the rest of the ingredients together. Mix, add dressing, and enjoy! This recipe is great for pasta, rice, couscous, and bulgur, and the dressing can be used on wild greens, too. The salad can be eaten hot for dinner or cool for the next day's lunch. Store in an airtight container if making lunch.

*Variations:*

- After pasta and vegetables have cooled, try adding about $1/2$ cup cubed cheese, $1/2$ cup chopped black or green olives, and $1/2$ cup cubed ham or pepperoni to give this salad an Italian flair!
- If you make the salad early on in your trip, you can substitute fresh ingredients such as onions, garlic, and peppers.
- For an added kick, add some hot sauce to the dressing.

## BASIC RICE RECIPE (SERVES 2)

    2 cups water
    $1/2$ tsp. salt
    1 cup rice (you can go with instant and reduce the simmering time)
    $1/2$ Tbs. margarine

Add salt to water and bring to a boil. Add rice and margarine and return to boiling. Cover and reduce heat. Simmer for 20–30 minutes.

**Hint:** When cooking rice or grains, put a spoon into the pot, gently push the grain aside, and check the bottom to see if the water has been absorbed. Do not over-stir, as it will become starchy.

## FRIED RICE

Cook rice as above. Melt margarine or put oil in frying pan. Add any spices such as curry, garlic, or salt and pepper. Fry rice until golden brown, 10–15 minutes. Do not overload pan, as it increases frying time.

## SWEET AND SOUR RICE (SERVES 3 OR 4)

Here is another good meal-in-a-bag!

    2 ½ cups water
    1 cup rice
    1 tsp. salt
    ½ cup raisins
    ½ cup other dried fruit, chopped
    2 Tbs. dried green and red peppers
    2 Tbs. dried onion (optional)
    ½ cup nuts and seeds
    ¼ tsp. black pepper
    2 Tbs. margarine

*Sauce (carry this from home already mixed):*
   ¼ cup water
   4 Tbs. vinegar (omitting removes
      "sour" element, but results are
      still good)
   3 Tbs. soy sauce
   3 to 5 Tbs. brown sugar or 3 to 4 Tbs. honey

Put water, rice, salt, raisins, peppers, dried fruit, and dried onion into a pan. Cook, covered, until rice is done. Drain if necessary. Add nuts and spices and fry in margarine 5–10 minutes.

For sauce, mix water, vinegar, soy sauce, and brown sugar together. Stir thoroughly into rice. Simmer a few minutes with the cover on. Serve.

*Variations:*
- Use ½ cup rice and ½ cup bulgur.
- Sweet and Sour Curried Rice: Add 1 to 2 Tbs. curry powder.

## CLAUDIA'S FAVORITE COUSCOUS PILAF (SERVES 4)

- 2 cups water
- 2 broth packets or 2 boullion cubes (vegetable or chicken are best)
- 3 Tbs. dried vegetables (peas, carrots, tomatoes, or mixed vegetables are good) or ½ to ¾ cup of sautéed fresh onions, garlic cloves, carrots and asparagus mix
- 1 cup dry couscous
- 3 Tbs. butter, margarine, or olive oil (or more to taste)
- ½ to ¾ cup finely cubed cheddar or jack cheese (do the cubing at home)

PREP at HOME

Bring water, broth, and dried vegetables to a rolling boil. Add couscous and margarine, stir well. Reduce heat, cover and simmer for 10 minutes. Check frequently, as it can burn easily. If you are using fresh vegetables, sauté them in another pan, starting with onions and garlic and then adding diced carrots and 1-inch spears of asparagus. This should take about 5 minutes. Once grain looks dry and light, remove from heat. Stir in cheese; cover for a few minutes until cheese is melted. Once fresh vegetables are done, add them to the grain and cheese mixture and serve with hot sauce, or curry.

**Note:** Margarine/butter/oil is the key ingredient to success for this recipe.

## BULGUR–RICE PILAF (SERVES 3 OR 4)

Makes a great meal-in-a-bag!

- 1 cup bulgur
- 1 cup rice
- 4 cups water (seasoned with any broth to taste)
- 2 Tbs. dried mixed vegetables
- 1 Tbs. dried onion
- 3 heaping Tbs. margarine
- $\frac{1}{2}$ cup cubed cheese

Add all ingredients except cheese to a pot. Cook, covered, over medium heat for 20 minutes. Stir as little as possible. When dry and fluffy, add cheese and scoop into oiled fry pan; fry until browned.

## TABOULI SALAD (SERVES 4)

Try this as a meal-in-a-bag!

- 2 cups bulgur
- 2 ½ cups boiling water
- 1 Tbs. dried onion
- 2 to 3 Tbs. dried mixed vegetables
- 1 mint tea bag (you may have one somewhere in your kitchen at home)
- 2 Tbs. parsley flakes
- ½ cup oil
- 1 tsp. salt
- ¼ to ½ tsp. pepper
- 5 Tbs. lemon juice (optional; vinegar may also be used)

Place bulgur, 2 cups boiling water, dried onion, and dried vegetables in a pot. Steep tea bag in remaining ½ cup water for 2–3 minutes. Discard tea bag and add water to bulgur. Let sit for ½ hour. Add remaining ingredients. Stir well. Allow to sit another ½ hour before eating.

## FRIED FISH (SERVES 1)

  1 cleaned fish, slightly wet, either whole or cut
     into steaks or fillets
  $1/4$ to $1/2$ cup cornmeal (white or wheat flour
     can also be used)
  $1/2$ tsp. salt
  black pepper, garlic powder, dill, dry mustard,
     or curry to taste
  oil or margarine for frying (oil gives better
     taste and crispness)

Mix cornmeal or flour, salt, and any desired spices in a plastic bag. Put in slightly wet fish and shake to coat. Remove fish and place it in hot oil or melted margarine in a frying pan. Fry slowly until fish is tender and flakes apart. Several cuts on the back of a whole fish or turning the fish frequently can prevent it from curling as it cooks.

*Variation:* Mix 1 Tbs. powdered egg with 2–3 Tbs. water and dip fish in this before coating with cornmeal or flour.

## BASIC FALAFEL RECIPE (SERVES 2 OR 3)

1 cup falafel mix
3/4 cup water
oil for frying

Stir water thoroughly into mix and allow to sit 10 minutes. Shape into small patties and fry on both sides in hot oil to desired crispness.

*Variations:*

- Serve with rice or pasta and a seasoned white sauce.
- Good with cheese melted on top.
- For a milder version, mix half falafel with half cornmeal or flour.

## BASIC POTATO RECIPE (SERVES 1)

1/3 cup potato pearls
2/3 to 1 cup boiling water
margarine to taste

Put pearls in a bowl. Add boiling water gradually until potatoes reach desired consistency. Stir in margarine.

*Variations:*

- Stir in grated or cubed cheese.
- Make potatoes with less water, form into patties, and fry in margarine. After turning, add slice of cheese to top and allow to melt. Good with hot sauce.

## MEXICAN-STYLE SPICY BEAN AND PASTA SOUP (SERVES 3 OR 4)

2 cups white pasta (macaroni, shells, and twists are great)

4 cups water

2 Tbs. dried green/red bell peppers

1 Tbs. dried onions

2 broth packets (or bouillon cubes will work)

2 Tbs. margarine

2 cups dehydrated black bean flakes or dehydrated refried beans

1 cup grated cheddar or jack cheese (do the grating at home)

PREP at HOME

hot sauce or salsa

black pepper, garlic, and chili powder to taste

Cook pasta, drain, and set aside. Separately, bring water, dried veggies, broth packets, and margarine to a boil. Add beans and stir. Turn heat down and simmer. Cook until beans are tender. Mixture should be brothy, so add more water if necessary. Cooking time depends on elevation. When beans are nearly done (the soup should have a gravylike consistency), add drained pasta. Add the grated cheese and hot sauce/salsa to individual portions. Serve with hot tortillas or bagels for dipping and spreading.

**Hint:** The black beans we use at NOLS are already preseasoned, so you may want to wait until the meal is cooked and tested prior to adding the last seasonings in the recipe.

## CHEESE BOMBS

A great meal-in-a-bag option.

    ½ cup flour
    ¼ cup baking mix (see p. 70)
    ¼ cup powdered egg
    ½ to 1 Tbs. or 1 packet broth
    ½ cup cheddar or jack cheese
      (cut it up small at home)

PREP at HOME

Mix all ingredients together except cheese. Add water until mixture is thicker than pancake batter but thinner than biscuit dough. Cut cheese in 1-inch squares about ½ inch thick. Dip in batter. Fry quickly on both sides in hot oil.

*Variations:* Popular seasoning combinations include 2 tsp. soy sauce, 1/4 tsp. dry mustard, and garlic; garlic, hot sauce or cayenne, and chili powder; or chili powder, cumin, and hot sauce.

## THUNDER CHILI (SERVES 3–4)

4 cups water

1/2 cup vegetarian chili mix or one small can of chili

2 cups potato pearls

crumbled or finely chopped cheese to taste (chop at home)

**PREP at HOME**

Boil water and add chili mix. Cook for 10–15 minutes. Take off heat, and mix in potato pearls until desired consistency is achieved. Add cheese to taste and stir until melted. Great alone or served with rice or tortillas, topped with salsa or hot sauce.

## SPOOZ-OLÉ (SERVES 3 OR 4)

Works great as a meal-in-a-bag!

MEAL in a BAG

    6 cups water
    2 to 4 Tbs. dried green and red peppers
    1 to 2 broth packs
    2 to 3 cups pasta (other than spaghetti)
    2 cups instant refried or black beans
    1 Tbs. dried onion
    1½ tsp. black pepper
    1 Tbs. garlic
    1 Tbs. oregano
    1 Tbs. chili powder
    ½ lb. or 1 cup cheddar or jack
        cheese (grate or cube at home)

PREP at HOME

Add peppers and broth packs to water and
bring to a boil. Add pasta and cook until tender. In
a separate container, rehydrate the beans, onion,
and spices with some of the boiling pasta water
until a gravylike consistency is achieved. Season to
taste. Drain the pasta and stir into the beans. Add
grated or chunked cheese, stir, and let melt.
Depending on the consistency you end up with,
you can either dip tortillas into it like a stew or fill
tortillas with the mixture and roll up and eat.

## VEGETARIAN MEATBALLS (MAKES 22–25 MEATBALLS)

A great meal-in-a-bag!

　　$^3/_4$ cup cornmeal
　　$^1/_2$ cup whole wheat flour
　　$^1/_4$ cup white flour
　　6 Tbs. dry milk powder
　　$^1/_2$ tsp. garlic
　　$^1/_2$ tsp. salt
　　1 Tbs. dried onion
　　1 tsp. soy sauce (check the fridge at home)
　　1 Tbs. oil
　　$^1/_2$ to $^3/_4$ cup water

Mix all dry ingredients together. Add rehydrated onions, soy sauce, and just enough water to make a stiff dough. Form 22 to 25 balls, approximately the size of a walnut. Add about 1 Tbs. oil to a fry pan and heat. Add balls and shake around until they are coated with oil. Cover and cook 20–30 minutes, shaking occasionally to be sure they brown on all sides.

**Note:** These can be served hot alone or on pasta, or eaten cold as a trail food.

# Desserts and
## SNACKS

O n the trail, as at home, a good meal
ends best with a little something
sweet. Desserts such as cookies and
GORP also make great trail food.

## NO-BAKE POWERHOUSE COOKIES
## (MAKES 20–24 COOKIES)

Do the prep at home!

PREP at HOME

    1 cup brown sugar

    1/4 cup margarine

    3 Tbs. powdered milk

    4 Tbs. water

    1 cup oatmeal

    1 cup peanut butter

    1/2 cup nuts

    1/4 cup chocolate or carob chips

    1/2 tsp. vanilla

Mix sugar, margarine, powdered milk, and water in a pan. Bring to a boil. Reduce heat and boil 3 minutes, stirring constantly to prevent scorching. Remove from heat and stir in remaining ingredients. Drop by spoonfuls onto a flat surface such as a pan lid. Let sit for about 10 minutes to set. In hot weather, they might not set as well.

## CHEWY FUDGE NO-BAKE COOKIES (MAKES 20–24 COOKIES)

1 cup brown sugar
$1/4$ cup cocoa mix
5 Tbs. margarine
3 Tbs. powdered milk
3 Tbs. water
1 $1/2$ cups oatmeal
$1/4$ cup nuts
$1/2$ tsp. vanilla

Mix sugar, margarine, cocoa, and milk (made from the milk powder and water) together in a pan. Follow same procedure as for No-Bake Powerhouse Cookies (above).

## NO-BAKE ESKIMO COOKIES
## (MAKES ABOUT 16 COOKIES)

Prep these at home, or whip them up
quickly in camp.

PREP at HOME

    1 cup oatmeal (instant or regular)
    6 Tbs. margarine
    6 Tbs. brown sugar
    3 Tbs. cocoa mix
    1/2 tsp. vanilla
    1/2 Tbs. water

Mix all ingredients together. Form into walnut-
sized balls. Eat immediately or let sit in a cool
place.

*Variation:* Roll in a combination of 1 Tbs. powdered milk and 1 Tbs. brown sugar, or in coconut.

## GORP

    1 cup shelled roasted and salted soy nuts
    1 cup salted peanuts
    1/2 cup butterscotch chips
    1/2 cup roasted and salted almonds
    1/2 cup roasted and salted cashews
    3/4 cup plain or peanut M&Ms

Mix all ingredients and enjoy!

## THE DELIGHT

This improvised dessert recipe was featured in *The Leader,* NOLS' alumni newsletter and was submitted by NOLS Pacific Northwest grads.

2 tortillas
$1/2$ Tbs. margarine
$1/2$ to 1 cup peanut butter
Handful chocolate chips
Handful brown sugar
Handful raisins
2 fig bars, crumbled

Place a tortilla smeared with peanut butter and sprinkled with chocolate chips and brown sugar in a buttered frying pan. Heat until the chips and sugar are melted; then top with raisins and two crumbled fig bars. Cover with another tortilla and fry until crispy. Slice and enjoy!

*Variations:*

- Try adding cranberries, granola, or peanuts.
- Flip the tortilla so that both sides become a little crispy.

**Hint:** Hold pan on top of windscreen so as not to burn tortilla.

# Appendix

**RESOURCES**

**www.nols.edu** (information about the National
    Outdoor Leadership School)

**www.nols.edu/pdf/lander/foodpricelist2.pdf** (price
    list for bulk food items at NOLS if you plan to
    come through Lander for a backcountry trip)

**www.maryjanesoutpost.org** (organic/natural alter-
    natives to premade backcountry food)

**www.unline.com** (two-ply plastic bags and spice
    bags)

**WEIGHT-BY-CUP**

For those foods you pack in bulk, the ounces per
cup listed here (for commonly carried items) should
help come up with an approximate weight:

| | |
|---|---|
| Almonds (shelled) | 5 ounces (oz.) |
| Cheese (grated) | 3¾ oz. |
| Cocoa (hot chocolate) | 4½ oz. |
| Coffee (ground) | 4 oz. |
| Corn meal | ⅓ oz. |
| Flour | 4 oz. |

| | |
|---|---|
| Margarine | 9 oz. |
| Milk (powdered) | 3⅓ oz. |
| Oats | 2¾ oz. |
| Oil (vegetable) | 7¾ oz. |
| Peanuts (shelled) | 6¼ oz. |
| Raisins | 5 oz. |
| Rice | 7½ oz. |
| Salt | 9½ oz. |
| Sugar (brown) | 6 oz. |
| Sugar (white) | 8 oz. |
| Tea | 2 oz. |
| Vinegar | 8 oz. |
| Walnuts (shelled) | 4 oz. |

## OTHER MEASUREMENTS

3 teaspoons (tsp.) = 1 tablespoon (Tbs.)
16 tablespoons = 1 cup (8 fluid ounces)
2 cups = 1 pint (16 fluid ounces and 1 pound)
2 pints = 1 quart (32 fluid ounces)
4 quarts = 1 gallon (128 fluid ounces)

# Index